DEVOTIONS FOR LENT 2015

 AUGSBURG FORTRESS

Minneapolis

GRACE & PEACE
Devotions for Lent 2015

ISBN 978-1-4514-9303-0

Writers: David L. Miller (February 18–25; March 28–April 4), Jennifer Clark Tinker (February 26–March 12), Jennifer Baker-Trinity (March 13–27)
Editors: Suzanne Burke, Laurie J. Hanson
Cover design: Laurie Ingram
Interior design: Eileen Engebretson

Manufactured in the U.S.A.

15 14   1 2 3 4 5 6 7 8 9 10

Welcome

Grace and peace! In Ephesians these are words of greeting, words of blessing, and, most of all, words to ponder. They are boundless gifts given to us by God through the life, death, and resurrection of Jesus Christ. These gifts empower us to live in the light of Christ and share God's grace and peace with each other and the world.

For each day in Lent 2015, *Grace & Peace* offers an evocative image, a reading from the letter to the Ephesians, a quotation to ponder, a reflection, and a prayer. Ephesians is the New Testament letter read most frequently in worship during this liturgical year (year B of the Revised Common Lectionary). The writers bring their unique voices and pastoral wisdom to these texts, and also offer the voices of other witnesses in the quotations they have chosen in the "To ponder" section for each day.

Images provide another way into these texts. Take time to wonder about the images. What do they say that words cannot?

Grace and peace to you as you journey through the days of Lent toward the Easter feast.

—The editors

February 18 / Ash Wednesday

Ephesians 1:3-6

Blessed be the God and Father of our Lord Jesus Christ, who has blessed us in Christ with every spiritual blessing in the heavenly places, just as he chose us in Christ before the foundation of the world to be holy and blameless before him in love. He destined us for adoption as his children through Jesus Christ, according to the good pleasure of his will, to the praise of his glorious grace that he freely bestowed on us in the Beloved.

To ponder

Well, you and I don't have to kill ourselves. We are the Beloved. We are intimately loved long before our parents, teachers, spouses, children and friends loved or wounded us. That's the truth of our lives. That's the truth I want you to claim for yourself. —Henri J. M. Nouwen, *Life of the Beloved*

Open hands

I stand at the table, my hands open to bless and offer gifts of bread and wine. But these hands are not really mine. They are your hands, Holy One, open to welcome and fill our emptiness with the fullness of a love that heals every doubt, fear, and wound.

You open your hands to give us everything that is in you—all the blessings of heaven that we might know the love you are and know ourselves as your beloved. Your hands tell me all my heart needs to know: I am wanted, chosen, forgiven, known, and treasured since before the dawn of time. And you fill me with the joy of knowing this because it brings you pleasure. Could it be . . . that I am your delight?

You tell me it is so. Little wonder that sometimes when I wake in the middle of the night, I repeat your name over and over. "Blessed," I name you. "Blessed are you, for you are the Love who fills my heart with the blessings of eternity. You stir my midnight prayer that I might know your open hands and praise the glory of your gracious heart."

Prayer

I am yours and you are mine, Loving Mystery. Let me live each moment in this awareness. Amen.

February 19

Ephesians 1:7-10

In him we have redemption through his blood, the forgiveness of our trespasses, according to the riches of his grace that he lavished on us. With all wisdom and insight he has made known to us the mystery of his will, according to his good pleasure that he set forth in Christ, as a plan for the fullness of time, to gather up all things in him, things in heaven and things on earth.

To ponder

The incarnation [of Christ] did not take place because of human sin. . . . Even if humans had not sinned, there would be an incarnation to bring creation to completion through the divine embodiment of Jesus. There is a creation so that there can be an incarnation of love, and the incarnation is God's embrace of creation, the human condition in particular. —Michael Blastic, in *Handbook of Spirituality for Ministers*, vol. 2

Tasting eternity

I feel the desire of your heart, Holy One. You yearn to gather us into loving unity with you. It brings you pleasure to share the substance of your life and love, your joy and beauty.

This is not a new plan or an afterthought. You did not set upon it as a way to repair creation after Eden's fateful fruit was picked, setting loose powers of fear and hatred, spoiling the beauty you had made. From the beginning—no, earlier—before the beginning, before the first spring breathed beauty on our flesh, before the first flower awakened us to wonder, before sunlight exploded into a spectrum of color through the first cloud, before the first rainbow, before . . . when there was only darkness and the mystery of who you are, your plan was already in place.

All things are destined to be joined into Christ. Every whirling element of this unimaginable universe will be gathered into one great unity, sharing your triune love. Every moment of loving unity we feel in this life is a foretaste of eternity, an incursion of heaven, moving us to laugh with delight and hope in every circumstance, bathed in the love you are.

Prayer

Open our eyes to see eternity in every instant of loving unity . . . and praise you. Amen.

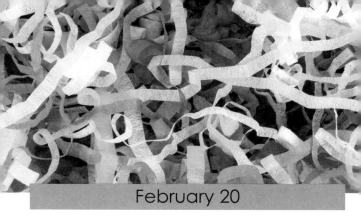

February 20

Ephesians 1:11-12
In Christ we have also obtained an inheritance, having been destined according to the purpose of him who accomplishes all things according to his counsel and will, so that we, who were the first to set our hope on Christ, might live for the praise of his glory.

To ponder

The enjoyment of God should be the supreme end of spiritual technique; and it is in that enjoyment of God that we feel not only saved . . . but safe; we are conscious of belonging to God, and hence are never alone. —J. S. Mackenzie, in *Finding God in All Things*

Our reality

How can I praise you for a love greater than any I thought I would ever know . . . or could know? How can I thank you for the startling joy that reality is better than my dreams and fantasies?

You lift us to praise every time we see and feel the reality into which we wake each day. Our little lives are strands in the story of your determined love, working in every circumstance to bring us into the joy of oneness with you and all that is. This is your holy dream, your eternal purpose. You have no desire to condemn or exclude. You treasure all you have made and hunger to draw all things into the love you are.

Our great sorrow and tragedy is that we so seldom see and know how profoundly we are loved and wanted, how significant our lives are, each contributing its unique texture and color to your great story.

So I wake each day and claim the truth that lifts us beyond our burdens into the joy of praising you, O God. Thank you for letting me be part of a great Love who will never let me go.

Prayer

Gracious One, lift us into the joy of praising you for the Love you are. Amen.

February 21

Ephesians 1:13-14

In him you also, when you had heard the word of truth, the gospel of your salvation, and had believed in him, were marked with the seal of the promised Holy Spirit; this is the pledge of our inheritance toward redemption as God's own people, to the praise of his glory.

To ponder

God almighty is our loving Father, and God in all wisdom is our loving Mother, with love and the goodness of the Holy Spirit, which is all one God, one Lord. And in the joining and the union he is our very true spouse and we his beloved wife and his fair maiden . . . for he says: I love you and you love me, and our love will never divide in two. —Julian of Norwich, *Showings*

You are mine, always

Thank you for your servant Simon, O Lord. Yesterday, I reached over the hospital bed and marked his forehead with the sign of the cross. I was as much blessed as he, maybe more. Never before have I served someone so distinguished. A Nobel Prize for physics graces his office for a lifetime of work I will never understand.

But that did not matter. He was dying and wanted the blessing I came to speak: "Simon, you have been sealed by the Holy Spirit and marked with the cross of Christ forever."

It's more than a formula. It is truth spoken to human souls at the very moment we realize we have no grip on life and never really did.

But it is so much more, O Lord. It is your voice . . . telling us not to fear, ever.

"You are mine," you told Simon. "You belong to me in every moment of your living and dying. I am yours, and you are mine . . . and you will always be. It doesn't matter that you can no longer hold on to your life, for I hold you."

We first hear this in our baptism. We need to claim it every day.

Prayer

Breathe your truth in our faltering hearts that we may know that we belong to you. Amen.

Ephesians 1:15-16

I have heard of your faith in the Lord Jesus and your love towards all the saints, and for this reason I do not cease to give thanks for you as I remember you in my prayers.

To ponder

To be . . . church . . . is to stand, shoulder to shoulder and hand in hand, precisely with people who are very different from ourselves and, with them, hear a common word, say a common creed, share a common bread, and offer a mutual forgiveness so as, in that way, to bridge our differences and become a common heart. —Ronald Rolheiser, *The Holy Longing*

The colors of love

I see the colors of love, Blessed One. Every four-year-old knows love is red and is shaped like a heart. They are too young to know that love encompasses every shade and hue we can imagine, every joy and sorrow we know.

We should color-code the notes on the prayer wall of our sanctuary. People stop there to write a prayer and stick it up on the wall. We could coat the wall with a great wash of color, the colors of love, blending every human need and emotion.

We could use red sticky notes for the loves that make us truly glad. Blue notes could speak our deep hopes and unfulfilled yearnings, white ones the joy of being alive and feeling free. Green or gold could lift prayers for healing, and scarlet the sorrows that won't heal.

Run all the colors together, each overlapping others, and you have the confusing, contradictory, mixed-up mess that is human life.

You also have one great visual prayer of thanks for the community of love and faith where every hue and color, every emotion and experience, is welcome in your love.

Prayer

Help us to be a community of love where all are welcome and hearts find healing. Amen.

February 23

Ephesians 1:17-19

I pray that the God of our Lord Jesus Christ, the Father of glory, may give you a spirit of wisdom and revelation as you come to know him, so that, with the eyes of your heart enlightened, you may know what is the hope to which he has called you, what are the riches of his glorious inheritance among the saints, and what is the immeasurable greatness of his power for us who believe, according to the working of his great power.

To ponder

At the corner of Fourth and Walnut, . . . I was suddenly overwhelmed with the realization that I loved all those people, that they were mine and I theirs, that we could not be alien to one another even though we were total strangers. . . . I almost laughed out loud. . . . I suddenly saw . . . what each one is in God's eyes. —Thomas Merton, *Confessions of a Guilty Bystander*

Revelation among the potholes

You open my eyes in unexpected moments, Holy One, that my heart may know you. Driving from Chicago's loop, the ramp bends right then a broad sweep left, descending into a south-bound merge lane on the Dan Ryan Expressway.

The city's northern skyline, alight in late afternoon sun, arrests my plunge into the rush-hour grind. Slowing to a crawl, my eyes caress the city's peaks, its streets and all who make this crazy place work. And I realize how much I love it all.

This love wasn't there a moment ago. But inner light illumines my mind and heart, and I know you. You are the Love who fills me and cherishes all that I see, the Love who is drawing the whole mess home into the love Christ is.

It is strange knowledge, not of the mind but of heart and intuition, awareness of an unnameable Love filling one's being and embracing all that is. It is knowledge of you, the God and Father of the Lord Jesus Christ, love's knowledge of you who made us for love and destined us to be united in love with all that is.

Prayer

Surprise us with the light of your love that we may live with unfailing hope. Amen.

Ephesians 1:20-21

God put this power to work in Christ when he raised him from the dead and seated him at his right hand in the heavenly places, far above all rule and authority and power and dominion, and above every name that is named, not only in this age but also in the age to come.

To ponder

The Mystery of Christ shines from one end of creation to the other; the whole shooting match is already lit up everywhere.... The church doesn't have to [get] ... people ... wired into Jesus. It just has to bring them the hilariously Good News that if only they will trust Jesus and open their eyes the darkness will be gone. —Robert Farrar Capon, *The Mystery of Christ*

The light of Christ

Your divine light, O God, explodes through the lens of the risen Christ, stretching to the outmost corners of the cosmos. You illumine the hearts and lives of every human soul in every place even where Christ's name is not known. He is the light of your divine heart, shining in every place and time.

There is no place where he is not.

Your heart, Holy One, is love and joy, compassion and wonder, blessing and grace shining on and in us amid the world's brokenness and our imperfections. Wherever grace and compassion touch human flesh, wherever wonder and love, trust and hope, kindness and joy appear . . . Christ is there, illumining hearts and drawing us into unity with you.

His light will permeate all creation and the depth of every human soul until there is nothing that does not shine with the light he is. All will bask in joy, sharing total unity with you, Loving Mystery. This is your holy purpose and deep desire.

Our yearning to know and be filled with your infinite love is but a mirror of your hunger for us.

Prayer

Illumine the dark sadness of our hearts that we may shine with you, the Love who never lets go. Amen.

Ephesians 1:22-23

And he has put all things under his feet and has made him the head over all things for the church, which is his body, the fullness of him who fills all in all.

To ponder

The man who is wise, therefore, will see his life as more like a reservoir than a canal. The canal simultaneously pours out what it receives; the reservoir retains the water till it is filled, then discharges the overflow without loss to itself. . . . Today there are many in the Church who act like canals, the reservoirs are far too rare. . . . You too must learn to await this fullness before pouring out your gifts, do not try to be more generous than God. —Bernard of Clairvaux, *On the Song of Songs*, Sermon 18

Filling the reservoir

I praise you in the morning hours for you are love unlimited, O God. You create every person and all reality out of love and for love. Is it any wonder we thirst to be filled with you, the Love who made us?

Sorrow endures, joy remains incomplete, and our souls ache until the reservoirs of our hearts are filled and spill over with your love.

It happens, though. Moments surprise when the heart is so full all sadness disappears, old hurts and wounds evaporate, and joy spills from every pore, watering the earth with divine life. These are moments of highest joy when we are filled with you and know the elation for which you intend us. Only then are we truly human, fully ourselves, and completely alive.

But daily frustrations and anxieties soon cloud our consciousness and the reservoirs of our souls drain dry. So we return to the places of filling, to people who love, to the church in all its imperfection yet through which the love of Christ flows, thirsty to be filled again with the fullness of the Love who is filling all things.

Prayer

Fill us with the love you are, that our souls may overflow and give life to the world. Amen.

Ephesians 4:1-3

I therefore, the prisoner in the Lord, beg you to lead a life worthy of the calling to which you have been called, with all humility and gentleness, with patience, bearing with one another in love, making every effort to maintain the unity of the Spirit in the bond of peace.

To ponder

Blest be the tie that binds our hearts in Christian love,
the unity of heart and mind is like to that above.
—John Fawcett, "Blest Be the Tie That Binds"

Truly bonded

Sometimes we avoid conflict to have the illusion of a "bond of peace." But then the difficulty between the parties is still unresolved and there is a restlessness under the surface. There is not peace when the problem remains unaddressed.

I once had a difficult clash with a friend from a different Christian tradition. She made an impassioned case against a common practice in my tradition. I took it personally and felt hurt. I tried to let it go, but I couldn't. I was not at peace. The bond between us was at risk. I finally made up my mind to address the issue privately with my friend. I approached as graciously as possible, choosing my words carefully, and simply described how I felt when she made her remarks.

She listened patiently and responded kindly, seeking to repair the rift. We had a very meaningful exchange. Even though neither of us decided to change our practice, we came to a better understanding of one another and our traditions. Our friendship—our "bond of peace"—was strengthened by our dialogue.

Prayer

Lord, help us to respond in grace as we maintain the "bond of peace" with one another. Amen.

February 27

Ephesians 4:4-6

There is one body and one Spirit, just as you were called to the one hope of your calling, one Lord, one faith, one baptism, one God and Father of all, who is above all and through all and in all.

To ponder

Each of us receives different gifts so that the body of Christ has what it needs to spread God's message of love. Note what this simple point really means. First, we all have gifts. . . . Biblically there is no doubt that we all have spiritual gifts and that each person and gift is important. Second, the gifts are given for the common good, not for the benefit of the individual who received them. We are simply stewards of the gifts we are given. —Jane A. G. Kise, David Stark, and Sandra Krebs Hirsh, *LifeKeys*

Different and united

One of my passions in ministry is vacation Bible school (VBS). As VBS director at my church, I look for a variety of different skills and gifts to round out the VBS staff. They could not be more different from one another in interests, abilities, and comfort levels with the kids. Even among those who choose similar jobs, different styles and personalities emerge as each person does the work in different ways.

When VBS finally arrives, I find that tapping into everyone's differences results in a beautiful whole. There is such engagement and laughter among the kids and staff! My heart is filled with awe that our work together brings such delight to all involved. We are unified in this ministry to bless the children of our community with the love of God in Christ Jesus.

On a larger scale, that's what our life is like as a community of believers. We are united in our baptism in Christ and equipped by the Spirit with a variety of gifts. All the gifts are important and each person plays a unique role for the common good as we bear God's love to the world.

Prayer

Lord, gather us all in you that we may be united in sharing your love. Amen.

February 28

Ephesians 4:7
But each of us was given grace according to the measure of Christ's gift.

To ponder
We confess that we are captive to sin and cannot free ourselves. We have sinned against you in thought, word, and deed, by what we have done and by what we have left undone. . . . God, who is rich in mercy, loved us even when we were dead in sin, and made us alive together with Christ. By grace you have been saved.
—Confession and Forgiveness, *Evangelical Lutheran Worship*

Overflowing love

I often feel so very undeserving of God's love—so captive to sin. Whether it is losing my temper with my son or worrying too much about being successful, one way or another I seem to find ways to devalue others and ignore God. Between what I have done and what I have left undone, I know that I can't get out of this mess by myself.

But the grace we receive is not grace according to how well we treat the people in our lives, or grace according to how impressive we are—it comes to us "according to the measure of Christ's gift." So what is that measure? It's self-giving, sacrificial, unconditional, overflowing love! Love so determined as to accept a death sentence for our sake. Love so powerful as to overcome death itself and rise victorious.

Jesus' love washes over us as he replaces our meandering ways with his persistent love. Because of our life in him, we too rise victorious so that we might share his love and grace in all that we do and say.

Prayer

Lord, grant us peace as we admit our need for you. Thank you for your grace and Christ's immeasurable gift of love for us. Amen.

March 1 / Lent 2

Ephesians 4:11-13

The gifts he gave were that some would be apostles, some prophets, some evangelists, some pastors and teachers, to equip the saints for the work of ministry, for building up the body of Christ, until all of us come to the unity of the faith and of the knowledge of the Son of God, to maturity, to the measure of the full stature of Christ.

To ponder

Every human is infinitely and equally valuable. We don't raise that value by achieving more than others. Our creator creates us equal. —David Housholder, *The Blackberry Bush*

Getting there

"Are we there yet?" My brother and I were excited about seeing the extended family waiting for us, and we couldn't wait to arrive at our destination.

Ephesians tells us that equipping believers and building up the body of Christ will bring all people "to the unity of the faith and of the knowledge of the Son of God, to maturity, to the measure of the full stature of Christ." All will believe in and know Christ and become like him.

God moves this vision forward through a variety of gifts that work together like spokes on a wheel. Some people preach and teach, while others share God's love primarily through their actions. Some people are visible to everyone. Others work behind the scenes. Each spoke on the wheel, however, is just as important and necessary as the next one in moving us toward our destination. We aren't there yet, but equipped with God's gifts to build each other up, grow in faith, and follow Christ, we are on the way.

Prayer

Lord, work in us and through us so that all may come to know you, be like you, and share your grace and peace with others. Amen.

March 2

Ephesians 4:14-16

We must no longer be children, tossed to and fro and blown about by every wind of doctrine, by people's trickery, by their craftiness in deceitful scheming. But speaking the truth in love, we must grow up in every way into him who is the head, into Christ, from whom the whole body, joined and knit together by every ligament with which it is equipped, as each part is working properly, promotes the body's growth in building itself up in love.

To ponder

Give us clear vision that we may know where to stand and what to stand for, because unless we stand for something, we shall fall for anything. —Peter Marshall, Senate chaplain, prayer offered at the opening of the session, April 18, 1947

Knit together

My favorite crochet projects involve squares. One square at a time is a finite and achievable goal for me and each finished piece gives me a sense of completion. Then, when I'm ready, I gather up the finished squares and join them together to form a larger whole that can bring more warmth and comfort than any one square alone.

It's tough to hold our ground, stick to our convictions, or face off with those who threaten to undermine what is important to us. We're likely to fall apart or unravel, particularly when we try to go it alone. But the fabric of our life together in Christ equips us and helps us to speak truth, grow in faith, and share God's love with others.

Prayer

Lord, knit us together with your grace and peace in Christ Jesus that we may cover the world with your love. Amen.

March 3

Ephesians 4:22-24

You were taught to put away your former way of life, your old self, corrupt and deluded by its lusts, and to be renewed in the spirit of your minds, and to clothe yourselves with the new self, created according to the likeness of God in true righteousness and holiness.

To ponder

Forgiveness gives us the capacity to make a new start.
—Desmond Tutu, *God Has a Dream: A Vision of Hope for Our Time*

Renewal

For me there is nowhere that my "old self" is more obvious than at home. I can't seem to stop myself from assuming the worst about what a family member says or does.

One day my husband was helping me work through a problem and suggested a way forward. I was irritated by the way he worded his advice, became defensive, and ranted. Exasperated, he interrupted me and acknowledged his bad choice of words. As we talked, I realized that my interpretation of what he said was not what he meant. I was upset with the man I love over something I had misinterpreted.

Especially at times like this, I wish I could be a more peaceful, more gracious, more loving person. I want to turn things around and make a new start, but how can I—how can we—do that? On our own we'll keep trying and failing. Where can we find "Seven Steps to a Better You" that will really work?

The writer of Ephesians would have us look to the cross, to the forgiveness and renewal made possible through the work of Jesus Christ for us. Because of these gifts of grace, we look with hope to the new things that God is working in us.

Prayer

Lord, renew us with your forgiveness to be reflections of your grace. Amen.

March 4

Ephesians 4:25

So then, putting away falsehood, let all of us speak the truth to our neighbors, for we are members of one another.

To ponder

I'd like to have a revolution of authenticity break out in the church where . . . we are forming authentic, true community . . . and that can only happen in telling the truth—in saying it like it is. —Mary DeMuth, podcast interview for *Life & Liberty Online Magazine*

Truth and community

When someone asks, "How are you?" what do you say? Most often we say "fine," but many times the truth is, we're not really fine.

I take a hard risk when I admit I'm not fine. First of all, I might sound like a complainer who doesn't appreciate the good things in my life. I might drag the other person down by talking about something that's bothering me. And there's also the risk of being misunderstood—or worse, being judged—for what is happening in my life.

But the reality is that everyone has ups and downs. Chances are good that the other person has had plenty of not-exactly-fine times too. When we leave the particulars—especially the challenges in life—behind a veil of secrecy, we are not fully known. When we risk telling our stories to one another, we can fully experience the love and acceptance that are possible even when we're struggling. Then true community can be formed.

Prayer

Lord, you are with us in all our ups and downs. Help us to be authentic with one another that we may know and build true community. Amen.

March 5

Ephesians 4:26-27

Be angry but do not sin; do not let the sun go down on your anger, and do not make room for the devil.

To ponder

I love that forgiveness helps us act completely different from what people expect. Instead of rage, we offer a bouquet of grace. Instead of bitterness, we walk in freedom. Instead of treating people the way they deserve (in our minds), we treat them better than we treat ourselves. This is forgiveness' beauty. —Mary DeMuth, *The Wall around Your Heart*

Standing up and stepping aside

Anger can arise quickly. A family member or friend says something hurtful to us. Another driver cuts us off in traffic. Someone we love dies from cancer. People who are homeless can't find shelter from extreme weather conditions. Nigerian girls are abducted simply because they want an education.

Whatever the reasons for anger, when we stuff it inside ourselves or take it out on someone or something else, it can have disastrous consequences for us, for others, and for the world.

There is another way, however. We can de-escalate a tense situation by working through an issue with respectful dialogue. We can join forces with others who want to put an end to cancer and other diseases, and get involved with organizations that work with people who are homeless. We can stand up for the rights of people in our communities, nation, and world. Instead of "making room" for further hurt or destruction, we can ask God to make room for grace and peace.

Prayer

Lord, make room for your grace and peace in our lives and in the world. Amen.

Ephesians 4:28-29

Thieves must give up stealing; rather let them labor and work honestly with their own hands, so as to have something to share with the needy. Let no evil talk come out of your mouths, but only what is useful for building up, as there is need, so that your words may give grace to those who hear.

To ponder

If you view your gifts as insignificant, remember that somewhere inside you is the image of God. God considers your soul a fitting home and wants you to think of yourself in that way as well. Your Creator has granted you the necessary resources to reflect back to the world all the love with which you were made. —Jane A. G. Kise, David Stark, and Sandra Krebs Hirsh, *LifeKeys*

I made it myself

There's something satisfying in looking at something I made with my own hands and knowing I made it myself. One hobby I enjoy is creating handmade books. I started out making a few blank books, then created books of handouts for retreats I led.

For my son's seventh birthday, I made secret code books as party favors. I chose four different codes and formatted the content on the computer. Then I photocopied the pages, cut the paper and covers to size, and hand-stitched the pages together to create pocket-sized booklets. They were a big hit with the kids at the party. My son, who is now ten, recently requested a second printing of the code books to share with new friends—the highest form of praise I could get for my handiwork!

Our actions and words make a difference. They can show someone that we care, and they can bring God's grace to others.

Prayer

Lord, guide our hands, our mouths, and all that we are to give your love and grace to the world. Amen.

March 7

Ephesians 4:30-32

And do not grieve the Holy Spirit of God, with which you were marked with a seal for the day of redemption. Put away from you all bitterness and wrath and anger and wrangling and slander, together with all malice, and be kind to one another, tenderhearted, forgiving one another, as God in Christ has forgiven you.

To ponder

Throughout the Bible, God first tells people who God is and what He has done for them. Only then does God state what God wishes people to do for Him—that they should serve God by serving others. —Harry Wendt, *The Divine Drama: The Biblical Narrative*

Developing kindness

Kindness isn't easy—especially when mischief can be so fun. I think particularly of the relationship I used to have with my big brother. As the older sibling he was better at everything— stronger and smarter than I, and the first to hit all the major milestones in life. But in one way I had power over him. I would sneak up on him at night just to see him jump and yelp. When he reacted on cue, I would burst out laughing. For a few brief moments, I had the satisfaction of having prevailed over my brother.

In time, I learned about the amazing tenderheartedness God shows to us, and gradually the jealousy I had as a kid toward my brother diminished and our relationship improved. I saw that God's relationship with us has nothing to do with power or showing anyone up, but is built on kindness, forgiveness, and grace through Christ.

Prayer

Lord, fill us with your kindness, forgiveness, and grace, that we may share these gifts and point people to you. Amen.

March 8 / Lent 3

Ephesians 5:1-2

Therefore be imitators of God, as beloved children, and live in love, as Christ loved us and gave himself up for us, a fragrant offering and sacrifice to God.

To ponder

Love is all about the other person. It overflows into service, not in order to show off how hard-working it is, but because that is its natural form. —N. T. Wright, *John for Everyone*

A good imitation

Young children can be such good imitators, copying the mannerisms, stride, and even the exact words of their parents and others around them. The problem is, we aren't always the best role models!

The writer of Ephesians calls us to be like children in imitating not other people, but God, and to love as Christ loved us. The love of Jesus took him to the cross, where he gave himself up as the sacrifice to end all sacrifices. This is a love without limits. What does it mean for us to imitate a love like this?

Some people have given up their lives for others, but most often we follow Christ's example in lots of little ways. Our self-sacrifice might involve parents setting aside their own needs to care for a child or caring professionals spending sleepless nights on call. It might include making the time to provide a listening ear for a friend or neighbor, or reaching out to someone we haven't gotten along with very well. It might mean standing up for someone who has been treated unjustly, or choosing to live beneath our means so we can give more to those in need. Motivated and empowered by God's love for us in Christ Jesus, we in turn love and serve others.

Prayer

Empower us, O God, and make us imitators of your love. Amen.

March 9

Ephesians 5:3-4

But fornication and impurity of any kind, or greed, must not even be mentioned among you, as is proper among saints. Entirely out of place is obscene, silly, and vulgar talk; but instead, let there be thanksgiving.

To ponder

Garbage in, Garbage out. —US Internal Revenue Service

Choices

When I was in elementary school, I started hearing "dirty" jokes. Part of me liked hearing about "grown-up" stuff that I knew I probably shouldn't be hearing. Before long I was repeating the jokes around other kids. Meanwhile, I started attending church and soaking up stories about God and growing in my faith. On one hand I was entertaining this raw humor and, on the other, wanting to draw closer to God.

Eventually I realized that, whether I wanted them to or not, the things I surrounded myself with often became a part of me. I began to have second thoughts about the things influencing me and the choices I had been making. Instead of more "garbage in," I could surround myself with people who would help me grow in faith and serve God and others.

Prayer

Set our minds on you, Most Holy God, that your grace and peace may flow out of us. Amen.

March 10

Ephesians 5:6-8

Let no one deceive you with empty words, for because of these things the wrath of God comes on those who are disobedient. Therefore do not be associated with them. For once you were darkness, but now in the Lord you are light. Live as children of light.

To ponder

I heard the voice of Jesus say, "I am this dark world's light;
look unto me, your morn shall rise, and all your day be bright."
I looked to Jesus, and I found in him my star, my sun;
and in that light of life I'll walk till trav'ling days are done.
—Horatius Bonar, "I Heard the Voice of Jesus Say"

Maximum exposure

During our senior year of college, under the cover of darkness, a fellow deaconess student and I snuck into our executive director's office and stuck glow-in-the-dark stars on her ceiling. It was all in good fun and she was good-natured about the prank, leaving the stars up for years after we graduated.

Not so harmless are the things we try to hide from ourselves, others, and God. These are the things we're ashamed of saying and doing, and things we should have said and done—but didn't. We'd like to have everyone remain "in the dark" about these things.

In order to turn us around, the light of Christ exposes these hidden things. The forgiveness of Christ washes away guilt and shame and calls us to walk in the light. With hearts and minds enlightened by Jesus and his love, we are transformed into children of light who carry the light of Jesus' love to others.

Prayer

Lord, shine in our hearts, that we might illuminate the world with your grace and peace. Amen.

March 11

Ephesians 5:15-20

Be careful then how you live, not as unwise people but as wise, making the most of the time, because the days are evil. So do not be foolish, but understand what the will of the Lord is. Do not get drunk with wine, for that is debauchery; but be filled with the Spirit, as you sing psalms and hymns and spiritual songs among yourselves, singing and making melody to the Lord in your hearts, giving thanks to God the Father at all times and for everything in the name of our Lord Jesus Christ.

To ponder

I set you apart in your right-now life for the daily work of liberation and love. —Sarah Bessey, *Jesus Feminist*

Spirit-filled

Wonder. Awe. Joy in the Lord. If only we could bottle the exhilaration we feel when we have a mountaintop spiritual experience. At Youth Encounter retreats in my teens, with many other Christian youth, dynamic speakers, and energetic musicians, I could feel the Spirit's presence. I wanted this experience to last forever.

But being "filled with the Spirit" doesn't mean a never-ending spiritual mountaintop experience. For one thing, that would get exhausting after a while. And there is much to do in "right-now life."

Day to day we can enjoy fellowship with other Christians, meditating on scripture and singing songs that help us center on Christ. Here and now the Spirit empowers us to notice what God is up to, receive God's goodness gratefully, and continually give thanks and praise to God. In our "right-now" lives, the Spirit brings wonder, awe, and joy in the Lord that last forever.

Prayer

Come, Holy Spirit, fill us and empower us to make known the grace and peace of Christ Jesus in our "right-now" lives. Amen.

March 12

Ephesians 2:1-3

You were dead through the trespasses and sins in which you
once lived, following the course of this world, following the ruler
of the power of the air, the spirit that is now at work among
those who are disobedient. All of us once lived among them in
the passions of our flesh, following the desires of flesh and
senses, and we were by nature children of wrath, like everyone else.

To ponder

Our nature has been so deeply curved in upon itself . . . that it
not only turns the finest gifts of God in upon itself and enjoys
them . . . it even uses God Himself to achieve these aims . . .
and it is even seeking God for its own sake. —Martin Luther,
Luther's Works, volume 25, *Lectures on Romans*

Getting on course

Martin Luther described sin by saying that we are "curved in upon ourselves," following our own needs and desires and doing everything for our own gain. Luther's words are as true today as they were in his time, but we describe things a bit differently. We say we're just looking out for "number one," getting all we can while the getting is good, and doing what we need to do to get ahead (even when we have to step on someone to get there).

The good news is that our God is a God of grace who does not leave us to get more and more wrapped up in ourselves. Through the life, death, and resurrection of Jesus, God turns our lives inside-out. God in Christ Jesus reorients us to be more loving and outwardly focused, following Christ and serving others.

Prayer

Gracious God, reorient our hearts and lives toward you and our neighbors, not for our own gain but so that all may know your love. Amen.

March 13

Ephesians 2:4-7

But God, who is rich in mercy, out of the great love with which
he loved us even when we were dead through our trespasses,
made us alive together with Christ—by grace you have been
saved—and raised us up with him and seated us with him in
the heavenly places in Christ Jesus, so that in the ages to come
he might show the immeasurable riches of his grace in kindness
toward us in Christ Jesus.

To ponder

For the love of God is broader than the measures of our mind;
and the heart of the Eternal is most wonderfully kind.
—Fredrick W. Faber, "There's a Wideness in God's Mercy"

Beyond measure

Measurements matter. When baking a cake, one carefully measures the ingredients to ensure proper texture and taste. A woodworker makes careful calculations before applying the saw. Some measurements are a matter of convenience; others can mean life or death. Has the surgeon pinpointed exactly where to make the incision? Have the architects, engineers, and contractors designed and built the structure to withstand natural disaster? We routinely trust our measurement skills and those of others in many areas of our lives.

Some might picture God as the supreme measurer, the one holding the yardstick, keeping track of how we are doing in this life. Have we measured up? Measuring may take us far in human affairs, but when it comes to the divine, measuring can falsely limit God, boxing the Spirit into our parameters. How often does Jesus take our human measurements and throw them out of proportion? Who is greatest? The least. Who is welcomed? The sinner.

Our measuring cups are finite; too much liquid and we will have a mess on our hands. Yet God's grace overflows, covering us with a kindness we cannot contain.

Prayer

Holy God, fill us this day with your grace beyond measure. In Jesus' name, Amen.

March 14

Ephesians 2:8-9

For by grace you have been saved through faith, and this is not your own doing; it is the gift of God—not the result of works, so that no one may boast.

To ponder

True humility does not know that it is humble. If it did, it would be proud from the contemplation of so fine a virtue. —Martin Luther, *Martin Luther's Christmas Book*

Who's best?

"Mom, Cassie thinks she is the best dancer in the class, but I know she's wrong. I'm the best dancer." So says my six-year-old son during a car-ride conversation. Thus begins a parent/child heart-to-heart about bragging.

What begins in childhood grows with us, this claim that our talents are all about us. Yes, talents need developing. Much like a garden seedling needs to be watered to grow into a healthy plant, a child hones a talent, adding to the innate gift hours of practice and a hearty dose of determination.

We teach our children to be proud of a job well done. Excellence gets rewarded with trophies and certificates. Yet faith is not like being the best dancer in the class. We might believe that having faith is a badge of honor. We might say, "Oh, that person has so much faith. Things will go well for her." But though we practice faith, it is not a merit-based gift. Faith is more like wildflowers dancing in the wind, growing without our planting but by the Spirit's bidding.

We leave grade school behind, but sometimes still it's best to take a backseat, look out the window, and give thanks for the gifts outside of us.

Prayer

Humble us, gracious God, that we exult in your goodness. Amen.

March 15 / Lent 4

Ephesians 2:10
For we are what he has made us, created in Christ Jesus for good works, which God prepared beforehand to be our way of life.

To ponder
The marvels of God are not brought forth from one's self.
Rather, it is more like a chord, a sound that is played.
The tone does not come out of the chord itself,
but rather through the touch of the Musician.
I am, of course, the lyre and harp of God's kindness!
—Hildegard of Bingen, in *Soul Weavings*

Making and being made

What do you make with your hands? With your mind? With your spirit? Though talked about separately, choral director Helen Kemp reminds us of the need for the whole self: "Body, mind, spirit, voice. It takes the whole person to sing and rejoice." At work or at play, our whole selves are brought before God, our creator.

As a musician, I've often used the phrase "making music." Perhaps you've said it too: "Do you see him over there, making music?" A dear mentor challenged me one day on this phrase. "We don't make music," he said. "Music makes us."

Hildegard and the writer of Ephesians knew this: God is drawing out our making, whatever this may be. Our callings, our vocations, are first about being aware of the goodness dwelling within us and around us: "And God saw that it was good" (Genesis 1:10, 12, 18, 21, 25). Sin and brokenness abound, tempting us to forget God's work within and among us, yet we are created for good. The challenge is hearing the Spirit, trusting that song of God flowing through us, and getting out of the way. Like baptismal waters, it is God's grace, making us into what God has called us.

Prayer

God of goodness, sing through our lives this day, creating us for good in the places we live and work. Amen.

March 16

Ephesians 5:10-14

Try to find out what is pleasing to the Lord. Take no part in the unfruitful works of darkness, but instead expose them. For it is shameful even to mention what such people do secretly; but everything exposed by the light becomes visible, for everything that becomes visible is light. Therefore it says,

"Sleeper, awake!
Rise from the dead,
and Christ will shine on you."

To ponder

I have learned things in the dark that I could never have learned in the light, things that have saved my life over and over again, so that there is really only one logical conclusion. I need darkness as much as I need light. —Barbara Brown Taylor, *Learning to Walk in the Dark*

In-between times

The choices seem simple: Do we come out into the light or stay in the darkness? Do we make a choice that exposes our neighbors or do we protect them? Yet we know the choices are more complex. Shedding light on a situation will cause harm to some, good to others.

We are simultaneously justified and sinful. We are justified by grace, the light of Christ. It is this light of God's goodness that shines through us, illuminating our way.

Yet we need darkness. In Lent, these lengthening days, we immerse ourselves in an awareness of death and darkness, not to be morbid or depressing, but to be honest that we are not all beams of sunshine. Darkness is real; it can frighten but it can also be the place for growth and discovery.

God will bring light from the darkness just as the dark earth yields springtime food and flower. But for now, we hover in these in-between times, between grace and sin, between light and darkness, between life and death. And in all these times, perceived or hidden, Christ's light shines.

Prayer

O God, awaken us to your grace whether we walk in darkness or light. Amen.

March 17

Ephesians 5:21
Be subject to one another out of reverence for Christ.

To ponder
Beloved, God's chosen, put on as a garment
compassion, forgiveness and goodness of heart.
Above all, before all, let love be your raiment
that binds into one every dissonant part.
—Susan Palo Cherwien, "Beloved, God's Chosen"

Bound in love

Ephesians 5:21 is immediately preceded by a passage about being filled with the Spirit and singing. Immediately following this verse we find counsel concerning domestic relationships.

Between church and home, this hinge verse calls us to community, for when we are bound to one another in love, Christ is revered.

How fitting that a verse commending being subject to one another follows an account of singing together. When we sing together, we are bound together by our breath, by singing the same words at the same time, and when not singing in harmony, we are united by a single melody. Dietrich Bonhoeffer notes, "It is not you that sings, it is the Church that is singing, and you, as a member of the Church, may share in its song" (*Life Together*, HarperOne, 2009).

Our lives in church and home will be dissonant; sin interrupts and we fail to listen to one another; we hear only our own voices. Yet God calls us to be subject to one another in the way Christ was subjected for us and for the whole world: in great love. In Christ's love, sung and shared, the dissonant parts of our songs and our lives are made whole.

Prayer

O God, make our voices whole by another's voice. Amen.

Ephesians 6:1-4

Children, obey your parents in the Lord, for this is right. "Honor your father and mother"—this is the first commandment with a promise: "so that it may be well with you and you may live long on the earth."

And, fathers, do not provoke your children to anger, but bring them up in the discipline and instruction of the Lord.

To ponder

The provision of care for children will proceed on a radically revised and improved basis if instead of seeing the child first as a problem faced with a complex of problems, we see her as mystery surrounded by mystery. —Martin E. Marty, *The Mystery of the Child*

Children of God

"Listen the first time. Remember your manners. Be kind to your brother and sister." These are just a few of the refrains heard regularly around our home. My hope as a parent is that my children obey these refrains because things indeed go better: less yelling, less mess, less hurt. But as anyone who has cared for children knows, things go awry. We all break promises.

Peruse a bookstore's parenting section and most books operate on this premise: children are a problem and this book will help you solve it. In response, Christian historian, pastor, parent, and grandparent Martin Marty calls us to a different premise: children are not a problem to be solved but a mystery surrounded by mystery. The gospel call to become like children (Matthew 18:3) is not a sentimental saying but a radical shift in our understanding of ourselves and of the mystery we call God.

Today's passage from Ephesians is a call to both children and parents. We are all children of God, washed in the same baptismal waters and immersed into the same mystery of Christ. How can we, washed into this mystery, live into it more fully as we care for one another?

Prayer

God of wonder, inspire our trust in your ways that are not our ways. Amen.

As Jesus' power was not only from God but with God, power is the gift of relationship with God and with the world God loves. We nurture this relationship in worship and service.

As people of faith, we trust that God's power is at work and that by such power, we are not only from God, but also with God. We are clothed in Christ, covered in grace, sharing in the power to bring hope from despair, life from death.

Prayer

O God, strengthen us by the power of your life-giving Spirit for the sake of all in need. Amen.

March 19

Ephesians 6:10-11

Finally, be strong in the Lord and in the strength of his power.

March 20

Ephesians 6:12

For our struggle is not against enemies of blood and flesh, but against the rulers, against the authorities, against the cosmic powers of this present darkness, against the spiritual forces of evil in the heavenly places.

To ponder

Redemption means actually being liberated from the oppression of the Powers, being forgiven for one's own sin and for complicity with the Powers, and being engaged in liberating the Powers themselves from their bondage to idolatry. The good news is nothing less than a cosmic salvation . . . when God will "gather up all things in him (Christ), things in heaven and things on earth" (Eph. 1:10). —Walter Wink, *Engaging the Powers*

Web of powers

On a sunny spring afternoon, my older children invited neighbor boys to play in the backyard. As I sat on the porch, ruminating on Paul's verses in Ephesians, they turned plastic baseball bats into swords and inflatable balls into bombs. The game is the classic: Good guys versus the bad guys.

Hence these six- and eight-year-olds set the stage for the dualisms that plague us in every season and at every age: good versus evil, strong versus weak, right versus wrong. As we mature we recognize, one hopes, that the enemies and powers have become more complex. Enemies are not only people with names, but systems wielding powers we can or cannot recognize. School boards, corporations, governments, family systems: we are caught up in a web of powers that can be forces for immeasurable good and horrific evil. In holy baptism, we renounce the forces of evil. We are forgiven; we are made new. With this newness comes the awareness of the forces that defy God, forces weaving within and among us. How will we live as Christ's people, as people charged to love our enemies—named and unnamed, within and without?

Prayer

Gracious Power, guide us as we live by your Spirit, trusting in your power to deliver us from all evil. Amen.

March 21

Ephesians 6:13-14

Therefore take up the whole armor of God, so that you may be able to withstand on that evil day, and having done everything, to stand firm. Stand therefore, and fasten the belt of truth around your waist, and put on the breastplate of righteousness.

To ponder

The armor of God is the embodiment, the internalization of the life of the Trinity—truth, righteousness, peace, faith, salvation, word of God—Christ in us, the hope of glory. Armor is redefined in terms of who we are, not in what we do. —Eugene Peterson, *Practicing Resurrection*

You are what you wear

The clothing industry wants us to buy into this truth whole-heartedly: you are what you wear. What we wear on the outside makes us or breaks us.

None of us can deny that clothes matter. We recognize paramedics by their uniforms, police officers by their badges. We recognize pastors, too, by their clerical garb.

This passage from Ephesians seems to be all about externalities, putting on armor, belts, and breastplates. But as with so much of scriptural language, this is metaphoric speech. The belt is a belt of truth, the breastplate, a sign of righteousness.

"You have put on Christ, in him you have been baptized" (*Evangelical Lutheran Worship*, 211). This baptismal refrain defies the fashion industry. Though we recognize others by their attire, what unites us is being clothed in Christ. As Eugene Peterson notes, "Armor is redefined in terms of who we are, not what we do." We take on many roles in this life. We wear many hats, but we are most fundamentally children of God, clothed in Christ, faith embodied. We pray to be covered in the care of Christ every day, dressed for success not as the world measures it, but in truth and righteousness.

Prayer

Holy God, cover us in your care that we may stand firm in faith. Amen.

March 22 / Lent 5

Ephesians 6:15-17

As shoes for your feet put on whatever will make you ready to proclaim the gospel of peace. With all of these, take the shield of faith, with which you will be able to quench all the flaming arrows of the evil one. Take the helmet of salvation, and the sword of the Spirit, which is the word of God.

To ponder

The devil specializes in providing anyone who will give him the time of day—he takes special delight in targeting Christians—with Technicolor, wide-screen versions of what it means to live a full life. . . . Meanwhile, we have a considerable number of witnesses in every generation who counter the devil's grandiosity and keep our ears close to the ground, our eyes on who or what is right before us, following Jesus in our own Galilees, practicing resurrection in our kitchens and backyards. —Eugene Peterson, *Practicing Resurrection*

Evil details?

"The devil's in the details." This cautionary phrase warns us to be alert, lest we miss the small stuff that could hijack a project. Eugene Peterson paints a different picture of evil for us, a picture not of smallness but of grandiosity. In the gospel accounts, Satan tempts Jesus with larger-than-life proposals, especially the temptation to give him "all the kingdoms of the world and their splendor" (Matthew 4:8). Evil can present itself in the temptation for more: more stuff, more prestige, more investments, and more and still more.

Peterson suggests that a way to resist the evil one is exactly in the details. While we are told and sold that we must have more, the more we really need might be right in front of us or walking beside us. Being ready to proclaim the gospel calls us to the ground: the ground of our being, of the land giving life to us, of the networks that hold us in their care. In the details we hear the still, small voice of God, promising life abundant, a "more" unlike any other.

Prayer

God, you are before us, with us, within us. For your presence in all things, we give you thanks. Amen.

March 23

Ephesians 6:18
Pray in the Spirit at all times in every prayer and supplication.
To that end keep alert and always persevere in supplication for
all the saints.

To ponder
The fruit and purpose of prayer is to be one with and like God
in all things. It is the will of God that our prayer and our trust
be large. We must truly know that our God is the ground from
which our prayer sprouts and that it is a gift given out of love.
Otherwise, we waste our time and pain ourselves. —Julian of
Norwich, *Meditations with Julian of Norwich*

Supply and demand

Supplication. You probably do not use this word in casual conversation, but you most certainly use its synonyms: asking, requesting, perhaps pleading.

If we consider prayer to be an ever-present connection to God, the ground of our being expressed in public worship and private devotion, supplication refers to a particular kind of prayer. We are supplied by the grace of God, but then we make demands: Help, O God, my friend who is dying. Help, O God, the victims of the flood. Help, O God, my addicted child. We are asking, requesting, pleading for God to act. This is supplication. Supplication mirrors a tree. When planted, a tree's roots spread, anchoring the tree more deeply. As the tree grows, the branches spread outward and upward. Asking out of our need, we are being extended for another. Even if we are unsure of God's love, we still come to God, begging for God's Spirit to work.

Prayer is a gift, the Spirit moving us to call upon God. It is supplied to us even when we think we are nothing but barren soil. Then, when we least expect it, we are drawn out of ourselves to God and to those for whom we pray.

Prayer

Supply us with your grace, O God, and hear us when we pray. Amen.

March 24

Ephesians 6:19-20

Pray also for me, so that when I speak, a message may be given to me to make known with boldness the mystery of the gospel, for which I am an ambassador in chains. Pray that I may declare it boldly, as I must speak.

To ponder

Let us be today's Christians. Let us not take fright at the boldness of today's church. With Christ's light let us illuminate even the most hideous caverns of the human person: torture, jail, plunder, want, chronic illness. The oppressed must be saved, not with a revolutionary salvation, in mere human fashion, but with the holy revolution of the Son of Man, who dies on the cross to cleanse God's image, which is soiled in today's humanity, a humanity so enslaved, so selfish, so sinful. —Oscar A. Romero, *The Violence of Love*

Holy revolution

We live in revolving times. This "we" is not only we who observe Lent this year. This "we" includes the earth and all its creatures. Our planet turns. Where there is light in one place, another place is covered in darkness. When one dies, another is born.

Christians make a bold claim of another turning, a claim Bishop Oscar Romero called "a holy revolution" and Ephesians calls "the mystery of the gospel." The claim is this: the world has turned in Jesus Christ. By the mystery of his incarnation, witness, crucifixion, and resurrection, the world has turned. This turning has not been fully realized, but fully promised. Followers of Christ pray to announce this promise boldly.

Paul and Romero lived in different times, but both felt called by the mystery of the gospel to live boldly. It could be speaking up when we are comfortable keeping silence or risking security to help a stranger. It could mean loving the unlovable.

The gospel promise that changes the world will change us. Sometimes it is easier to be enslaved in fear. Yet the mystery of the gospel calls us to embrace the holy revolution revealed by God through Jesus by the power of the Holy Spirit.

Prayer

O God, turn us to you in bold prayer and bold living. Amen.

March 25

Ephesians 6:23-24

Peace be to the whole community, and love with faith, from God the Father and the Lord Jesus Christ. Grace be with all who have an undying love for our Lord Jesus Christ.

To ponder

Peace within the church still dwells
in our welcomes and farewells
and through God's baptismal pow'r
peace surrounds our dying hour.
Peace be with you, full and free,
now and through eternity.
—Nikolai F. S. Grundtvig, "Peace, to Soothe Our Bitter Woes"

The parting word

The letter to the Ephesians ends as it begins, with words of grace and peace. Centuries later many of us conclude formal letters or cursory online notes with one word: "peace."

Some doorways display doorknockers or plaques with these words: "Peace to all who enter here." It seems that there should be a similar sign behind the door inscribed with the words often heard at the communion table and the funeral liturgy: "Depart in peace." In words and in actions, peace conveys the fullness of arriving and departing.

Such peace surpasses contentment. Comings and goings, birth and death, will be far from content. Midwives and hospice workers care about peace, but such peace will not be complete absence of pain. Rather these people bring a caring presence in the midst of our labors.

The peace that Christ brings when he finds his disciples hidden behind locked doors is not a vague contentment but his Spirit meeting their pain and fear. This is why peace can be full and free even in the hour of death. This parting peace is not what the world gives but what God in Christ gives by the touch of his Spirit who dwells in and among us.

Prayer

In our endings and beginnings, gracious God, surround us with your peace. Amen.

Ephesians 2:12-13

Remember that you were at that time without Christ, being aliens from the commonwealth of Israel, and strangers to the covenants of promise, having no hope and without God in the world. But now in Christ Jesus you who once were far off have been brought near by the blood of Christ.

To ponder

Hospitality means primarily the creation of free space where the stranger can enter and become a friend instead of an enemy. Hospitality is not to change people, but to offer them space where change can take place. It is not to bring men and women over to our side, but to offer freedom not disturbed by dividing lines. —Henri J. M. Nouwen, *Reaching Out*

Outside the lines

We learn at an early age how to form lines. Preschoolers line up and follow their teacher. Children and adults line up to eat, to buy, or to ride. When we are far off in a line, unable to see its end, we grow impatient, irritated. Lines force us to wait and keep us from getting on with whatever else we'd like to be doing. Those other people are in the way.

At what point do we discover that we are all in line together and make peace with our fellow line-standers? Can we accept their company, perhaps even strike up a conversation? If something has delayed the line, can we have compassion? Or are we stuck behind "others," those strangers we must pass in order to get ahead?

The physical space between you and another might be a few feet, but we form distances far greater in our hearts. Whether it is how we treat someone in the grocery checkout or those beliefs we hold about who's inside or outside of God's grace, we forget that we have all been brought near. Christ stands outside the line, welcoming us all to holy space.

Prayer

Christ our way, be known to us and through us, in the lines of our lives and beyond. Amen.

March 27

Ephesians 2:14-16

For he is our peace; in his flesh he has made both groups into one and has broken down the dividing wall, that is, the hostility between us. He has abolished the law with its commandments and ordinances, that he might create in himself one new humanity in place of the two, thus making peace, and might reconcile both groups to God in one body through the cross, thus putting to death that hostility through it.

To ponder

Love recognizes no barriers. It jumps hurdles, leaps fences, penetrates walls to arrive at its destination full of hope. —Maya Angelou, Facebook post, January 11, 2013

Keeping the peace

"Truly I tell you, not one stone will be left here upon another; all will be thrown down." So announces Jesus in Matthew's gospel (Matthew 24:2). Jesus is referring to the temple walls, walls that would eventually fail.

Up to a point, boundaries help. Some would like to see a border fence built between the United States and Mexico. Will it keep the peace? Or like other walls humans construct, the Berlin Wall, for example, will it ultimately fail?

Walls provide shelter, fences delineate property, all in attempts to clarify where we stand in the world. Yet when we put our ultimate trust in such boundaries, they become our idols. Our trust is in what we have made and our peace a product of our well-laid plans.

Jesus' promise to be our peace is an end-time announcement that transforms the walls. In the cross, Christ has broken every barrier down. The walls of the tomb could not hold him. This is the promise begun yet not fully realized. For now, we keep on building and trusting in walls and, yes, working and praying for peace. In humility we confess that ultimately we do not keep the peace; Christ keeps us.

Prayer

O God, bring peace surpassing our buildings and boundaries. Amen.

March 28

Ephesians 2:17-18

So he came and proclaimed peace to you who were far off and peace to those who were near; for through him both of us have access in one Spirit to the Father.

To ponder

Jesus invites us, in this life, in this broken, beautiful world, to experience the life of heaven now. He insisted over and over that God's peace, joy, and love are currently available to us, exactly as we are. . . . There is heaven now, somewhere else. There is heaven here, sometime else. And then there's Jesus' invitation to heaven here and now, in this moment, in this place. —Rob Bell, *Love Wins*

Jesus is our peace

It happens every time we gather. Words are spoken: "The peace of the Lord be with you." "And also with you" comes the reply.

With that, worshipers move around, crossing the aisle, making lots of noise, looking for people to greet and bless. Once they were careful and constrained. Now they dive in, playfulness having replaced polite restraint. The warmth of physical and emotional unity fills the room.

On good days, I lean against the baptismal font at the front of the church and savor the moment. I want time to stop amid the joy and blessing being shared in not so peaceful ways. It's a vision of your holy kingdom, O Lord.

So many things separate and divide human souls. In the ancient world, Jew and Gentile were worlds apart, one near to God, the other thought to be far off. Today, even our schedules separate us, making us strangers to God and each other just as assuredly as our prejudices, politics, and mistrust of those we don't know.

But you are our peace, my brother, coaxing us into a great sea of peace and blessing where what is shared is the love you are.

Prayer

Fill us with the Spirit of your peace that we may bless across the divides of our lives. Amen.

March 29 / Sunday of the Passion

Ephesians 2:19-22

So then you are no longer strangers and aliens, but you are citizens with the saints and also members of the household of God, built upon the foundation of the apostles and prophets, with Christ Jesus himself as the cornerstone. In him the whole structure is joined together and grows into a holy temple in the Lord; in whom you also are built together spiritually into a dwelling place for God.

To ponder

True brilliance is the glory of God transforming each and all of us into sons and daughters of the Father through Christ in the Spirit, bonding all together in a communion in the one Love.
—Michael Downey, *Altogether Gift*

The household of my love

I ache to belong, Holy One, but I am hardly alone. Loneliness and hidden pain endure until we enter loving unity with others where nothing in us is strange or alien but welcome.

We cannot create such a community. Our differences stir insecurity. We draw lines and build walls to exclude those whose ways and ideas threaten our own. Political and moral convictions divide us into competing camps, hardening hearts and blocking love from flowing beyond the narrow confines of "my people," "my friends."

Every time our differences create aliens and enemies, Christ suffers assault. For you are building a holy temple, a household where all are welcome and our differences are joined in loving union.

"Surrender your fears of each other," you say. "Drop the self-righteousness that hides your uncertainty. Cease pretending that you are something more or less, stronger or weaker than others. It is not true. You are just human and needy, hungry for my love. Trust and know, my love is your home. You will find freedom to share the joys and suffering, the beauty and wisdom of other human souls in the household of my love."

Prayer

Wash away our hurts and hatreds, our fear and mistrust. Build your household of love among us where all may abide. Amen.

March 30

Ephesians 3:1-4

This is the reason that I Paul am a prisoner for Christ Jesus for the sake of you Gentiles—for surely you have already heard of the commission of God's grace that was given me for you, and how the mystery was made known to me by revelation, as I wrote above in a few words, a reading of which will enable you to perceive my understanding of the mystery of Christ.

To ponder

Many people have come to believe through their contemplation that Jesus desires their friendship and companionship even more than they desire his. And the desire is not utilitarian. That is, Jesus does not desire their friendship only because he needs workers in the vineyard. Jesus wants friends and companions.

Just as he reveals himself to them, so too he wants them to reveal themselves to him . . . a friendship that is mutual. —William A. Barry, *Finding God in All Things*

Have no doubt

I cannot imagine you, Holy One. I try to grasp your glory with words and images, but you are constantly beyond my reach. I cannot take hold of you, so I fall silent and listen to the mystery of Christ speaking in my depths.

"I have come that all might be one in me," you say. "When I am lifted up I will draw all things into one love. It is my desire for you to find wholeness and peace in unity with me. All that I share with the heavenly Father, the fullness of life, the intimacy of eternal love, is intended for you and all creation.

"I tell you this because you are my friends, and I hunger for you to know the mystery of who I am and what I am doing, so joy may fill you and create in you a new and loving heart. I give vision to my prophets and apostles that they may open your eyes to see that I am drawing all you are into my love. Nothing and no one is to be lost to me."

Prayer

Fill us with clear vision of the mystery of your will that we may live in hope and serve with joy. Amen.

March 31

Ephesians 3:5-6

In former generations this mystery was not made known to humankind, as it has now been revealed to his holy apostles and prophets by the Spirit: that is, the Gentiles have become fellow heirs, members of the same body, and sharers in the promise in Christ Jesus through the gospel.

To ponder

The wisdom and power of God are evident in the concrete experience of church life as very different people are joined in grace to hear a common word, share a common bread, offer mutual forgiveness, and be joined in a common heart, filled with the love of Christ. —David L. Miller, *Ephesians: Leader Session Guide,* Books of Faith series

A sacrament of God's dream

I give thanks for your church, blessed Christ. Lord knows, it's not perfect. It has frustrated and disappointed me for decades. But there are moments when we shine with your beauty in simple and unassuming acts.

Wednesday night, the book club moved its meeting to be with Peggy. She'd fallen, broken bones, and landed in rehab, so they took their meeting to the rehab center lest she feel alone, forgotten, or unimportant.

I doubt they understood the significance of what they'd done. They were a sacrament of your holy dream, knowing the unity of being joined in your love.

Every week we gather to pray and sing, to share our food and lives, to serve the poor, keep up the church, and dozens of other things. Each time we are moved beyond our separateness into a unity of praise and love, joy and purpose.

There are Republicans and Democrats, conservatives and progressives, NRA members and those who hate guns, successful people who earn great sums and others who are just getting by; a mixture of ethnicities is sometimes apparent too.

We are one, a living expression of the loving unity you are weaving in all creation.

Prayer

Make your church a living witness to one love, which is your will for all things. Amen.

April 1

Ephesians 3:7-8

Of this gospel I have become a servant according to the gift of God's grace that was given me by the working of his power. Although I am the very least of all the saints, this grace was given to me to bring to the Gentiles the news of the boundless riches of Christ.

To ponder

What is this strange and elusive thing we call love? Quite simply, it is life pouring itself forth. To say that "God is love" is to say that God is not enclosed, turned in on self. God is the life that pours itself forth constantly, abundantly, excessively, never-to-stop-coming-as-gift. —Michael Downey, *Altogether Gift*

Boundless riches

Two words resonate in my soul, Loving One, and I yearn for them to fill me and chase everything else from my heart. So I repeat them again and again, "boundless riches, boundless riches."

This is your name. This is who you are. The constant beat of your gracious heart sends your love coursing through all creation, capturing our hearts so that we long to be carried away in the rhythm of your life.

You are always enough, always more than we expect or imagine. The boundless riches of your heart seek the saddest corners of human life and our hidden pains that we may know you . . . and know . . . you are unlike anything we have ever known.

We know all that rises falls, every beauty fades, every joy wanes. Every soaring song whose rhythm lifts us high too soon dies away.

But not you. You are boundless. You reach to the end of time and beyond. No great sin or wound of my troubled soul is beyond your reach, your loving and healing compassion. Nothing is beyond you, for you are boundless riches.

Prayer

Let my heart bask in your boundless riches that I may feel what it means to be alive. Amen.

April 2 / Maundy Thursday

Ephesians 3:14-17

For this reason I bow my knees before the Father, from whom every family in heaven and on earth takes its name. I pray that, according to the riches of his glory, he may grant that you may be strengthened in your inner being with power through his Spirit, and that Christ may dwell in your hearts through faith, as you are being rooted and grounded in love.

To ponder

Every part of us is, at its core, a desire for love's fulfillment. Our senses seek the beauty, the sweetness, the good feelings of God. Our mind seeks the truth and wisdom of God. Our will seeks to live out the goodness, the righteousness of God. Our imagination seeks the justice and peace of God. . . . Human beings are two-legged, walking, talking desires for God. —Gerald May, *The Dark Night of the Soul*

Hunger for union

Sometimes my soul grows weary and sad when I do not feel your nearness, only separation and distance. I need you. I need to know you, my Lord, planted deep in the soil of my soul, reviving my heart with joy and hope.

So I bow and cry out to you. I do not seek new ideas or concepts about you. They weary me. I seek only you, hoping to feel your love in my inmost soul enfolding and consoling my heart, bringing me the joy and peace beyond all want and unfulfilled longings.

Morning comes, and I come to you once more, sinking deep into my soul, crying out whatever pain or joy I feel within. And a miracle happens. My pain becomes your presence, and this burning hunger for union is satisfied.

I fly on the wings of prayer into the soul of who I am and find you waiting there for me to arrive, crying out for me, loving me, inviting me to rest . . . and know you as only lovers know.

The feeling of your absence is overwhelmed by the truth that you are the love who is always present within me, hungry for me to come home.

Prayer

Move me to tears of joy this day, the joy of knowing you. Amen.

April 3 / Good Friday

Ephesians 3:18-19

I pray that you may have the power to comprehend, with all the saints, what is the breadth and length and height and depth, and to know the love of Christ that surpasses knowledge, so that you may be filled with all the fullness of God.

To ponder

Very simply, love is the core of everything. . . . It is the sole purpose of all creation and of us as human beings. And it is, finally, impossible to distinguish precisely whether this love at our center is our love of God, or God's love of us, or our love of ourselves and one another. . . . If we are made of love, filled with love, why do we feel so separate . . . ? We are asleep to the truth and do not realize who we are and what we are for . . . [and] we become attached to things other than God. —Gerald May, *The Dark Night of the Soul*

Knowing the unknowable

You open your arms, Jesus, in one great divine embrace of all that is and all that I am. You exclude no one and leave nothing out, no shame or guilt, no failures or unfulfilled longings.

Heart wounds cry out in the night for your presence to fill the emptiness and grant that peace we cannot give ourselves. And you are there, your arms open, whispering, "Come to me."

Is it true? Can our wounded souls be filled with the fullness of you who are the life of all that lives, the love of all that loves?

Yes, I know . . . and even when I forget, somehow I still know, remembering moments when my heart brimmed with the fullness of a love I cannot fathom. It is then that I know the unknowable. I hold that which all heaven and earth cannot contain.

Fill me again with all that you are, Loving One. I will never understand you or how it is that your fullness comes to me. But it does, and I know it is your joy to fill me. So fill me again. My forgetful heart needs to know . . . you.

Prayer

You made us as vessels to hold you, blessed Christ. Fill us with the fullness of you who are filling all things. Amen.

Ephesians 3:20-21

Now to him who by the power at work within us is able to accomplish abundantly far more than all we can ask or imagine, to him be glory in the church and in Christ Jesus to all generations, forever and ever. Amen.

To ponder

The first experience that has to be mentioned is the feeling of rapturous joy. When the Spirit of the Resurrection is experienced, a person breathes freely again, and gets up out of the defeats and anxieties of his or her life. . . . We begin to love life with the love of God. . . . Peace is another experience of God's Spirit in our restless souls: peace with God in Christ, and peace because . . . we experience how deeply the love of God has been poured into our hearts. —Jürgen Moltmann, *The Source of Life*

One love

I fall on my knees in wonder at the staggering complexity of your love at work in all I see. The night sky reveals a universe filled with light, color, and staggering stretches of darkness. On Easter Vigil, and every night, the heavens are lit by billions of stars in billions of galaxies, their light racing across light-years of space to delight my eye and move me to wonder.

You said, "Let there be light!" and light exploded, shattering the darkness. Everything that has happened since are facets of one great story—the story of how you continue to shatter the darkness and draw every blessed thing into union with your love, Holy One.

This is your plan and promise, and your church, drawn together by the love of Christ, is a foretaste of the unity of love and color, beauty and joy you are creating.

Glory to you, Holy One, for your plan and promise to draw all that we see and are—all that is and will be—into one love, the love of Christ that no death can defeat.

Prayer

You created the world to be one holy communion in your love. Unite us and all that is in the triumphant love of Christ. Amen.

Notes

February 18: Henri J. M. Nouwen, *Life of the Beloved* (Crossroad, 1992), 30. **February 19:** Michael Blastic, "Attentive Compassion: Franciscan Resources for Ministry," in *Handbook of Spirituality for Ministers*, vol. 2, ed. Robert J. Wicks (Paulist, 2000), 257. **February 20:** J. S. Mackenzie, "Nervous Disorders and Character," quoted in William A. Barry, *Finding God in All Things* (Ave Maria Press, 1991), 31. **February 21:** Julian of Norwich, *Showings* (Paulist, 1978), 293. **February 22:** Ronald Rolheiser, *The Holy Longing* (Doubleday, 1999), 115. **February 23:** Thomas Merton, *Confessions of a Guilty Bystander* (Doubleday, 1966), 179–80. **February 24:** Robert Farrar Capon, *The Mystery of Christ* (Eerdmans, 1993), 65. **February 25:** Bernard of Clairvaux, *On the Song of Songs*, Sermon 18, "The Two Operations of the Holy Spirit," www.pathsoflove.com. **February 26:** John Fawcett, "Blest Be the Tie That Binds," *Evangelical Lutheran Worship* (Augsburg Fortress, 2006), Hymn 656. **February 27:** Jane A. G. Kise, David Stark, and Sandra Krebs Hirsh, *LifeKeys: Discover Who You Are* (Bethany House, 2005), 76. **February 28:** Confession and Forgiveness, *Evangelical Lutheran Worship*, 95–96. **March 1:** David Housholder, *The Blackberry Bush: A Novel* (Summerside Press, 2011), 159.

March 2: Peter Marshall, US Senate chaplain, prayer offered at the opening of the session, April 18, 1947. **March 3:** Desmond Tutu, *God Has a Dream: A Vision of Hope for Our Time* (Image, 2005). **March 4:** Mary DeMuth, podcast interview for *Life & Liberty Online Magazine*, October 15, 2013, http://www.davidhousholder.com/0241-life-liberty/. **March 5:** Mary DeMuth, *The Wall around Your Heart: How Jesus Heals You When Others Hurt You* (Nelson Books, 2013), 160–161. **March 6:** Jane A. G. Kise, David Stark, and Sandra Krebs Hirsh, *LifeKeys*, 31. **March 7:** Harry Wendt, *The Divine Drama: The Biblical Narrative*, participant manual (Crossways International, 2004), 73. **March 8:** N. T. Wright, *John for Everyone*, part 2, chapters 11–21, (Westminster John Knox Press, 2004), 56. **March 9:** US Internal Revenue Service article syndicated in the US about the first stages of computerization, April 1, 1963. **March 10:** Horatius Bonar, "I Heard the Voice of Jesus Say," *Evangelical Lutheran Worship*, Hymn 611. **March 11:** Sarah Bessey, *Jesus Feminist: An Invitation to Revisit the Bible's View of Women* (Howard Books, 2013), 195. **March 12:** Martin Luther, *Luther's Works*, volume 25, *Lectures on Romans* (Concordia Publishing House, 1972), 291. **March 13:** Fredrick W. Faber, "There's a Wideness in God's Mercy," *Evangelical Lutheran Worship*, Hymns 587/588. **March 14:** Martin Luther, *Martin Luther's Christmas Book*, ed. Roland H. Bainton, (Augsburg Books, 1997), 20. **March 15:** Hildegard of Bingen, in *Soul Weavings: A Gathering of Women's Prayers* (Augsburg Books, 1996), 70. **March 16:** Barbara Brown Taylor, *Learning to Walk in the Dark* (HarperOne, 2014), 5. **March 17:** Susan Palo Cherwien, "Beloved, God's Chosen," *Evangelical Lutheran Worship*, Hymn 648. **March 18:** Martin E. Marty, *The Mystery of the Child* (Eerdmans, 2007), 1. **March 19:** Mary Jo Leddy, *Radical Gratitude* (Orbis, 2002), 98. **March 20:** Walter Wink, *Engaging the Powers: Discernment and Resistance in a World of Domination* (Fortress, 1992), 83, 85. **March 21:** Eugene Peterson, *Practice Resurrection: A Conversation on Growing Up in Christ* (Eerdmans, 2010), 263. **March 22:** Eugene Peterson, *Practice Resurrection*, 275. **March 23:** Julian of Norwich, *Meditations with Julian of Norwich*, ed. Brendan Doyle (Bear & Co., 1983), in *Soul Weavings*, 139. **March 24:** Oscar A. Romero, *The Violence of Love*, trans. James R. Brockman (Orbis, 2004), September 23, 1979 homily. **March 25:** Nikolai F. S. Grundtvig, "Peace, to Soothe Our Bitter Woes," *Evangelical Lutheran Worship*, Hymn 381. **March 26:** Henri J. M. Nouwen, *Reaching Out: The Three Movements of the Spiritual Life* (Image, 1986), 51. **March 27:** Maya Angelou, Facebook post, January 11, 2013. **March 28:** Rob Bell, *Love Wins* (HarperOne, 2011), 62. **March 29:** Michael Downey, *Altogether Gift: A Trinitarian Spirituality* (Orbis, 2000), 77. **March 30:** William A. Barry, *Finding God in All Things* (Ave Maria Press, 1991), 96. **March 31:** David L. Miller, *Ephesians: Leader Session Guide*,